WHY OUR CUSTOMERS QUIT?

GERALD A. LONG

authorHOUSE™

1663 LIBERTY DRIVE, SUITE 200
BLOOMINGTON, INDIANA 47403
(800) 839-8640
WWW.AUTHORHOUSE.COM

First published by AuthorHouse 12/05/05

ISBN: 1-4259-0642-7 (e)
ISBN: 1-4208-9441-2 (sc)

Library of Congress Control Number: 2005910655

Printed in the United States of America
Bloomington, Indiana

This book is printed on acid-free paper.

TABLE OF CONTENTS

Acknowledgments:

A special thank you goes out to my wife (Rosemary), who has inspired and corrected me along the years to keep me going in the right direction. Also my kids (Erin, Aimee, and Andrew), who have supported and assisted in many parts of my life and career. Not to mention the putting up with me as I complain about the problems in the service industry today.

I couldn't have written this book without my career in the restaurant business, particularly Subway (the franchise). A special thanks to Fred Deluca and Dr. Buck along with their staff at Doctors Associates, Inc. I can't forget the development agents that I have met and worked for over the years; Wayne and Joe and their staff have been an inspiration as well as leaders who have pushed me to start something I really enjoy. With all of these people I have learned the secrets of being successful in business, and have had the opportunity to develop my skills in speaking on these topics that I am so passionate about. There are many franchisees whom I have met and worked with over the years. The trials and tribulations that we encountered together were what helped me understand that it takes customers to make our business move, and it is how we take care of them that makes us succeed long term.

The most important people I have to thank are those people who have pushed me over the edge and shown me there is a need to talk to people about their business and how to be good at it. This includes all of those working in retail establishments, hair salons, and restaurants who I have had the opportunity to visit, and in whose businesses I have seen memorable services (good and bad). I have my share of places that I have quit going to, I have some that I call my favorite place, and those few who have gotten that second chance and have won me back. I will refer to some of these places as examples, but mostly as a category so as not to single anyone out. There have been some awesome experiences, and I actually have written a lot of them down with the intention of sharing as many as I can. I would like to show you what these employees or employers are doing to keep their businesses growing, or to keep their customers coming back!

Another Special Thank You goes to John Hokanson and his partner Pat Christiansen. Both of whom have given me the opportunity to understand and direct the other side of a full service restaurant. I used this concept (Why Our Customers Quit!) to develop a restaurant and staff that better accommodate the customers who keep the restaurant open.

Thank You ALL!

PREFACE

Where did they go?

Last year's business was so good. This year sales are down a little (or a lot). Yes, we have some new competition, but why is it so slow?

Or, maybe you are just the person who has a business and it is good enough. *I only work this hard, actually it gets easier and easier every year, but I put this much in my pocket!*

This is a chance to find out where your customers are going, or where they went. *We have new faces come into our business, yet the sales are still flat. Do I have enough business? Is there more? How do I get it?*

More importantly—*How do I keep the people I have worked so hard to get?*

Why Our Customers Quit is a book and also a presentation for people who own a business, to help them understand the little things that help a customer decide where they want to go, and why they choose to come back.

Every year we have people who quit coming to us for reasons we cannot control. Either they move away, they change their habits, or they die! These are customers we have to replace. The bigger problem is the customer who leaves due to an attitude of indifference. About 66% of your customers who have quit coming have quit because they had a disagreement that was not resolved.

Why was it not resolved? Maybe we were not looking for the problems?

If you can't see a problem, you can't fix it!

Let *Why Our Customers Quit* open your eyes to the many things that your customers see and feel when they experience your business. Let us help you to open your eyes to customer indifferences!

Author's Note

My name is Gerald Long. I am a general manager of a very busy full-service restaurant. My restaurant career started very early in life; my stepfather had excellent cooking skills, and I wanted to take that same direction in my future endeavors. I attended a local culinary class at a community college in town. Upon completion of high school and the culinary class I went to the Culinary Institute of America for continuing education classes.

After a job as an executive chef for six years, I was tired and wanted to do something fun. I joined a team of consultants that guided restaurant owners in running their businesses. We worked with the famous sandwich chain Subway. Twelve years later my wife and I owned a few of the franchises and I have continued to share knowledge of this franchise and how to be successful at it. I enjoyed this part the most. Over several years, I realized my strength was teaching and leading those who wanted more! I had experiences with several people who had spent their hard-earned money, and in some cases their life savings, on a business, and they had no idea what to do. I found out one very important thing as I was guiding these people. This was the concept of "why we do what we do?"

Why we do what we do? ~ When we are training if take the time to explain to the newly hired employee why we do things a certain way, why it is important to our business, this combined with how it should be done will give them a better understanding of why we do what we do?

When an opportunity came to hold a seminar I jumped up and volunteered to do my part. My focus was that people pay money to get into business, and if they are not good at it then they would be out of business, and soon! With this focus I decided that more and more people needed to know what happens to their business when their most prized commodity—the customer—is not taken care of. They quit!

Working in the restaurant business, you find that your nights and days off are often spent at a restaurant, eating. We have been to many places over the years, and have seen some ideas that would make people rich, but unfortunately we saw many more ideas that are making people poor! The sad thing is someone has spent a lot of money to get into a business of their own, and by not being aware of some important facts they can soon be out of business. Okay, on a smaller scale maybe they are just losing profits because they are losing some of their business?

I started to make mental notes of the things I had seen, and I felt this would be a great workshop! The problem is most people who speak have a book. So I set out to collect more data to write my book, *Why Our Customers Quit.* This is a manual on how to see problems in our own business and what it will take to keep the customers coming back to us. This book was going to be a book for restaurant employees, managers, entrepreneurs, and franchisees. Then my wife said these same principles apply to anyone's business. Take care of your customers or someone else will! So we started collecting information for a broader group—Any business with customers or clients!

So we now have a concept that all of you in the business world who take care of people daily need to see.

I still have the passion to speak. My friends will tell you that I can! I want to share this same concept with stakeholders (employees and management). I want them to realize that they are the most important part of customer satisfaction and customer retention. I have turned the concept of workshops into a fun environment called "Fun Shops."

Please visit our Web site, www.OurCustomersCount.com, to learn more about the printed materials and Fun Shops we offer, or to book a date for that next meeting

Sincerely,

Gerald A. Long

1: What's the Problem?

So, we want to know where our customers are going? In the following pages you will learn the six categories of where customers are going, and most of all why they quit! (Or should I say quit coming to us for food, hair care, or other services.)

What Do You Need to Do?

Step 1: Acknowledge that you have an opportunity to improve.

Step 2: Assess where your problem lies.

Step 3: Share with the employees what the problems are, what role they play in correcting them, and how they will benefit from getting them turned around. It is important that everyone understands that they have a role to play in this, and that everyone has something to benefit by getting it turned around. From the server at a restaurant who gets tipped out based on their performance, to the hourly employee who gets hours and pay for their contribution, they all have something to gain. Employees are not employees if the employer does not stay in business. You offer them a place to work, and they control whether or not your revenues (customers) return!

Step 4: Train, train, train—You know there is room for improvement, you looked at your business and saw what the problems there are, and you now need to work on improving those issues. You spoke to your staff, and shared the concerns, and then you told them how this involves them; now you need to show how to correct the problems.

I learned a three-step process for training that I have stuck with and feel that I have done well with: *Show-Tell-Involve*. We have to *show* them the way, *tell* them how it needs to be done, and *involve* them in trying and implementing it. With this process we can use role playing to show how it is done and what the results can bear.

Step 5: Measure your success. Don't be afraid to ask, how did we do today? Was everything okay? Was that the way you wanted it today? Sometimes we don't want to know the answer, but need it to proceed to succeed.

Step 6: Repeat. Just like the famous shampoo line, lather, rinse, and repeat, this is an ongoing process.

You will hire people who will excel at this, and there will be those who have potential to get there. This is your business! If you fail, you lose! (A lot!) So if you don't select the right people you *can* lose. Another catch phrase is "Hire the attitude and train the skill." This means hire the person who is bubbly and out-going to be the greeter or hostess for your business. She or he will make that first and lasting impression a memorable one. Because you may not get a chance to talk to me or read a book on hiring the right person for the job, I feel the need to elaborate on this.

When a person applies for the important position you are trying to fill, do they meet the characteristics that the position requires? Never thought of it that way? For example, a receptionist should be friendly, outspoken, and should like people. Would you hire a person with the hobbies of watching TV or playing video games as this person? I would look for the person who was involved with school activities and was in clubs. The key questions that we ask at an interview are what tell us if that person can be trained to complete the task. As I told many franchisees in my customer service workshops with Subway, hire the attitude, you can teach anyone to make a sandwich!

Remember, train, train, train!

Numbers Don't Lie!

Have you thought about it this way: If we were to lose one customer a day for an entire year, what would that mean to our business? This does not take into consideration who each person may come in contact with and what they will say! Please look at both examples and see what is really happening:

Example #1: A dinner house with an average check of $15 loses a customer every day. If that customer brings one person with them we lose $30 in business each day. For the year we lose $10,950.

If we put 20% to the bottom line (Profit), then we missed an opportunity to add $2,190 to the bottom line. (What if this restaurant has 50 or more employees? Did they lose three today?)

    1 Customer + 1 Guest = 2 Customers X $15 = $30

    $30 lost each day X 365 = $10,950

    $10,950 Sales X 20% Profit = A Loss of $2,190

Example #2: A quick-service restaurant that does mostly lunches and has an average check of $6 loses a customer every day. If we put 22% to the bottom line, then we missed an opportunity to add another $963 to the bottom line.

    1 Customer X $6 = $6

    $6 lost each day X 365 = $2,190

    $2,190 Sales X 22% Profit = A Loss of $482

(Don't forger an unhappy customer tells a few people and that number can grow!)

And this may not be the total loss! Remember:

- They could tell others!

- They could eat with others in their family or business and not bring them back there!

- They could be gone for two to three years . . .

Year One we lost $ 10,950 Sales ~ $2,190 Profits

Year Two we lost $ 32,850 Sales ~ $6,570 Profits

Year Three we lost $ 54,750 Sales ~ $ $10,950 Profits

And so on . . .

2: WHERE DID THEY GO?

This was shown to me by a person who was passionate about training, and I have used it in many of my opportunities to share with others. (Thank you, Linda Serabian.)

WHY OUR CUSTOMERS QUIT

1% Die

3% Move

5% Find other friends

9% Go to our competition

14% Are dissatisfied with product or service

68% Experience an attitude of indifference of an employee to the customer!

So, NOW THAT WE KNOW WHERE THEY ARE GOING, HOW DO WE CHANGE THIS VICIOUS CIRCLE?

Well . . .

1% Die: We cannot change this cycle. We need to be looking to feed this cycle to get new customers in to fill the voids we have.

3% Move Away: Again, this is something we cannot change. If they move to another neighborhood, or even another state, their habits will change and no longer involve us. These customers too have to be replaced to fill this void. It is also important to note that habits change, and take people away from us. For example, there is a mom who takes her child to school in the morning, then goes to the dry cleaner, and our business is next door. Well, we got her by chance and we kept her. But now that her child is in grade school and takes the bus, mom does not do her errands the same way. We lost another!

5% Find other friends: Well, we were doing a great job, but they just stopped coming. This person may have found a new friend. Yes, there is a new employee who came to work, and they like to go to X instead. We lost that person to a different clique!

9% Go to our competition: I remember too many times when a hard-working Subway owner was afraid of losing his business to a competitor. Well, when you are a giant, people want part of the pie. When we received notice of the competition's plans to come into the market, I always warned them that if we do a great job in-house then we will only experience a small setback. Sure the customers will want to try the new guy, and see what is special, but if we treated them well then they will be back! (When I say special I mean John, Bob, and Gary Special. Not just the Norm.)

14% Are dissatisfied with product or service: So they didn't like that sandwich, or the way they were treated. We can fix this, but is it too late? We lost some people, so we need to make sure that we are doing what they expect! This is when we have to ask those taboo words: How was your lunch? How did we do today? We may not like the answer, but by asking we do two major things. First of all, we find out what people do not like and we can set a course to try to remedy the situation. But, more importantly, we asked and showed that we care what they think! This means we will probably get a second chance to make that impression.

How can we get them to tell us? We have to ask! A comment box will help. Make it accessible and encourage the use. I have offered a free lunch to the best idea for improvement. This box should be available for guests and employees alike. I use the box as a sounding device for employees to post suggestions, and monthly we use it to allow employees to select the employee of the month.

** LET ME PAUSE TO DO A SELF-PROMOTE! **
I have spoken on three topics in my life, and local marketing is the second! This is an opportunity to get my next book, Am I Fishing in the Right Pond? This book is about proven methods for getting people to fill the voids or vacancies that we have. We all have ideas, and the salespeople that come in to sell you say we reach this many people, they may not be the right choice! Marketing can be fun, and does not have to be costly. Check it out!

IF WE DO NOT ASK, THEN THEY MAY NOT TELL!

You probably have heard many statistics that did not sound too accurate, but I want to share one that I strongly believe in: For every one person who shared something (a comment) there were ten more who were too busy or too shy to take the time to share. I went through the drive-thru for a quick breakfast fix during my long drive into work. I was constantly disappointed by the employees' inability to get my order accurate. This was one of the largest burger chains, and they must be losing customers by the day! I occasionally would break my disgust and give them a second, third, fourth chance. It was this last time that I said enough is enough and called to voice my aggravation. Now let me share. I, like most people, eat breakfast every day, and in my car during my hour drive is quick and easy. So the first exit has the place I would like to go. If I order the cinnamon rolls they forget the icing, if I order the bacon sandwich I get the sausage. It seems to me that they grab whatever is there to fill the order. I don't want to get off on this . . . I will later!

After at least six or seven disappointments I finally decided someone had to be told, and I called. Up until then, I was one of the quiet ten people who did not speak up.

When you see customer counts or sales drop, you need to evaluate your business to see "how are we doing?"

That's it. We lose all of those customers due to the above reasons!

Wait! What about the remaining 68%?

That is the largest part, and probably the area where we can make the most impact!

68% of our customers quit due to an attitude of indifference of an employee to our customers!

This will be hard to explain, or hard for some to understand, so I will show some examples. This may spark a memory of what you have seen as a consumer that made you feel this way, or maybe an experience when you saw an employee with your customer that may have turned them off . . . or made them quit!

In a meeting not too long ago a coworker shared a saying that I have now adopted and used. (Thanks, Lisa Shipman, for making me aware of this.) "A person's perception is their reality."

What does this mean? To put it in other words, if that is how the customer sees it, then in their mind that is how it was. If the customer says it is cold in here, then they are cold. If they feel that it is too noisy, then to them it is too noisy. We cannot convince them otherwise, we can only try to fix the situation. Never argue with their perception. You can't win, you will just offer an attitude of indifference. In some cases you cannot make a change to satisfy the customer, but taking the time to listen may be enough!

When a customer is sharing, do your best to *just listen*! We may not have the answer now, and may need to get back to them. We may need to get a higher decision. But, by listening, we let them know they have been heard.

EXAMPLES:

- Employee locked the door early, and when the customer pulled on the door, instead of letting her in he just walked away!

- Employees, in uniform, were behind the counter, but not taking care of the guest!

- Employees were talking about their plans or past experiences versus listening to the customers they were taking care of.

- An employee gave a customer a cup to fill with a soda, and the cup had a leak. The customer asked the employee for another, but the employee only knew the rule that the cups were counted and if you used an extra one you would be charged for it. So did the customer get a new one? Sorry!

- A customer was waiting a long time for service and asked a passing server for help. "This is not my station!" was the response!

- In a restaurant I saw an employee who was making loud noises that were inappropriate. Even though the restaurant was closed, there were still customers nearby being disturbed. The sad thing about this is the employee did not feel like it hurt him at all. He wasn't waiting on the customer! Sadly, if this customer quit, then he hurt the server whose tip may have been reduced, he hurt the business sales from loss of income, but what he didn't see is that the restaurant offers a certain number of customers a day, and in their rotation he gets every sixth customer. If he reduces the restaurant's customer counts by causing them not to return, then he loses his share as well!

- Recently at the movies nearby, we ran in to catch a new release. Since sales are slow at this theatre, the concession sells tickets on slower nights. The person working the counter (who had a manager nametag on) was talking to a friend. We stepped over to the next line where they only sold the concession items. We bought our drink and popcorn, and then continued to wait for the conversation to end. Since we were already running late and previews were near the end, we had to move quickly. After about three more minutes we left. The sad thing is if he feels like this did not hurt him, then he too does not see things through! When business is slow we have to make sacrifices. In the restaurant business we get fewer hours to schedule our employees. Sometimes we lose good people who want more hours. Maybe had this not been the practice, the manager may have had higher sales, and would not have had to be manager, ticket seller, and ticket taker all in one? I am not knocking the need to cross train and make our business more efficient, but **we have to take care of our customers, or someone else will**!

Once as I was planning a presentation someone shared a new view that I had not heard. He said that customers are like sheep and our employees are like wolves. The employees eat the customers, or kill them off one at a time. This may be harsh, but we have to look at things on a larger scale to realize we have problems. I have seen many business owners who have gotten comfortable. They have this much business, and they make this much money! It's good enough! This book is for them, but they will not read it, never mind buy it! It's a shame.

Another old saying and again I do not know who said it first:

Rule #1 The customer is always right!

Rule #2 When #1 does not apply, refer back to Rule #1

3: Where Does My LOGO Go?

In this book we cover many different examples of why customers quit coming to our businesses. We learn that what happens inside our restaurant can determine whether or not the customer will return, and if so how often. The problem is that sometimes we lose a customer before they ever make it to our business. We may never get the chance to make the first impression. Actually we already did get a chance; it was not a favorable one. But when? How?

Let me explain!

In your business you wear some sort of uniform, or at least a nametag with the company name or slogan on it. This is a great way to market your business on what I like to call roaming billboards. However, it is not always positive advertising. When people are wearing your name on their bodies then their actions will make a statement about your business.

You have to be aware of the people you hire, and how they carry themselves. You need to have a plan as to how they have access to your logo, and when they will be able to use it.

What brought this to my attention and made it a necessary item to add to this book was a trip to the local mall. A group of kids were sitting near us at the food court. Two of them were wearing uniforms from a food place that is common in a lot of malls. They were sitting with their friends, talking loudly and using foul language. In their group there were people burning themselves with lighters, and they were talking about how they do bad things to the food people are going to eat. Now we all know that kids like to talk, and they are often going to say things just to be cool. The bad thing is they just turned off some people who will probably tell others. They didn't say where they worked, but since they had the logo on their shirts it was easy to decipher. These young people made an impression on many potential customers without even getting their business.

A few more examples:

When I was first asked to take over the restaurant I work at, I decided to make a trip down to secret shop* it, and see what needed to be done. When I arrived it was during the dinner rush. As I arrived I saw two employees outside who were smoking. As we entered the restaurant there was a small wait at the podium. My first impression was, why are they outside and not taking care of the customers? There could have been a few good reasons why, but the important thing is, in the eyes of the customers who were waiting, these were employees who should have been helping them. Remember, perception is reality!

- Secret Shop ~ When you send someone to patronize your business and get a performance review on how the visit was.

My first duty as general manager was to eliminate all breaks during peak hours, move employees on breaks to the back of the building, and last of all to only allow them to go out one at a time. I have a unique philosophy when I manage. The customers come first, and if what I see makes a poor impression on the restaurant, then it is my chief objective to change it. I told the servers I would correct things to help them make more money! Keep in mind, if they make more money so does the business.

It may not always be something they like, but it will be what it takes to make customers happy. This is what it takes for them to make more money.

The following is my goal and should be yours as well: Be aware of and fix all bad impressions that are made in our businesses. Now, there are things that customers will see that we cannot change, and this is part of doing business. But always be looking for ways to make a better, more favorable impression to your guest

I also saw a few other things happening that to some people may have seemed okay, but to me they made a poor impression. Our restaurant is pretty busy. We will usually have seven to nine servers working. As business slows down, people are cut from the floor and they start to do their work to leave. During this process they do not have customers in their stations, but there are customers in the restaurant. How these employees act will affect the customers' visit to the restaurant, as well as the tip for the servers waiting on them. I had to control loud noises, foul language, horse playing, etc.

At another store, employees were arguing over who was going to take the customers at the door because they wanted to be cut! This could happen in any business, but it happened in mine just once! I then had a meeting to share what had been seen, what it does to our business, and also that anyone who was seen or heard of doing any of these things would be let go. We take care of the customers; if we don't someone else will!

TAKE CARE OF YOUR CUSTOMERS,

Your Customer

OR SOMEONE ELSE WILL!

Your Competition

4: Take Care of Your Customers

We have to take care of our customers, or someone else will! So the question is how to improve or eliminate the customer indifference? It is not easy, and it will take a lot of time and training.

Step 1: Evaluate your current status and needs.

Step 2: Schedule a meeting with all of your stakeholders.

Step 3: Have a Fun Shop. Train. Try role playing with plenty of examples of what to do, and what not to do. Show, tell, and involve. Tell them why we do what we do.

Step 4: Inspect what you expect. Okay, we made changes, and we told everyone how to do it, so is it being done?

I used three catchphrases that are key to success in development (training) of employees:

Why We Do What We Do:

I have shared this with everyone who I have ever taught to be trainers in our business. It is easy to say, "Do this because of the book, or even better because I said so!" I have learned over the years that an employee will remember how to do something if we take the time to tell them why we do it that way! Sometimes we have to make up something, because no one else did! When I was a franchisee for Subway I had to hire people to make sandwiches. I had to train them on how much of each ingredient to use and in what sequence we needed it placed on the sandwich. I remember that the first item was onions and then the lettuce. We told them that the onions went on first because it flavors the meat! Then the lettuce because it holds the onions down; the other items were due to the color and eye appeal of the sandwich. Remember that if it looks good, it will taste good. Don't forget the famous "you taste with your eyes first"!

Another helpful example is the explanation for why the coolers must be kept shut. This is because bacteria multiply much faster in the danger zone, which is 41–150 degrees. This sounds serious so I better do it!

Show, Tell, and Involve:

In my training I always learned by being told to do something. When I read about the how, I had a better understanding, and then I took it all in when I was thrown into the fire and had to do it. So why not incorporate this into the training process? Tell them how to do it (and why!), then show them how to do it, and finally, let them try it, and correct it if needed. Retention will be greater!

Inspect What You Expect:

We trained them! Are we done? No! We need to make sure that the person we hired understood and is executing. The saying "Inspect What You Expect" should be printed over every work area in every business. If you do not check your results you may not know if you are getting the results you strive for!

PERCEPTION

Or

REALITY?

Facts:

#1: Between 50% and 74% of customers who share a complaint will do business with you again if the complaint is acknowledged!

#2: This number jumps to 95% if it is resolved quickly!

#3: Resolution is often just listening to the customer and thanking them for taking the time to share with you!

2 YEARS AGO

ONE YEAR AGO

SIX MONTHS AGO

TODAY

5: Complaints and Complainers

I know someone would like to ask this next question, so I will bring it up and yes, talk about that problem!

It is inevitable that someone will come into your line of business and not be happy. In fact, there are some people who plan to visit and try to get something for free.

Let's talk about the people who are unhappy and what they can mean to your business. There are people who come into your business and, like the people who quit, they are unhappy with the food, service, atmosphere, variety, etc. . . . We have one advantage with this customer compared to the one who quits! They have stayed to tell us why they are not happy.

This is an opportunity!

This is someone who has taken their time to tell you that things are not quite right today! We do not know right away if this is legitimate, so we do not know how to respond. Here are some keys to sorting out information from an unhappy customer:

#1: Listen.

Most often when someone has taken their time to let you know, they just want to be heard! Sometimes just having someone be the sounding board and thank them for their time and information is all people want. They just want to be heard, and they want the feeling that someone is going to do something about it! So if all else fails, listen!

#2 <u>Do not judge.</u>

This is done so often, and usually done by the employee before the manager or owner gets to the table to see the guest! For example, I have a customer at table X who is not happy with his dinner. He looks like a homeless person, and probably just wants something for free! So you, the manager/owner, go to the table with the pre-conceived notion that he is not going to eat here for free, and then tell all other homeless people! It should be your game plan to arrive at the table with an open mind, and more important, open ears. A polite greeting will set the mood for the input. "Hi, my name is . . . How can I help you this evening?"

#3: <u>Do not take it personally</u>.

A woman comes in and she is frustrated. She asks for a simple request and a quick drink. You offer something else and she gets annoyed with you. "I said this and a drink!" You start to take it personally and you want to say something back. Don't! You do not know this person, nor why they have this attitude. It could be because she has been treated rudely before, or maybe her car is broken down on the side of the road, and she is waiting for help and does not want to miss them. Sometimes we don't know why people act the way they do, but do not take it personally, because they could have it a lot worse than you! Who knows? She may offer a reason for her demeanor and you may be able to offer assistance in return. "Would you like to use the phone to call someone?" This could not only turn this situation around, this is also going the extra mile. She will remember when someone cares and is sincere in helping her. She will be back!

#4: <u>Set policies or standards.</u>

Have a game plan! When I visit a table I know that I do not want to give money back. But, I do want a happy person that will be back, and will tell others how well he was treated today. So, how can I do this? Listen and have a plan to make it right. A customer who is in a hurry and was unhappy with their meal may not have time to wait for the meal to be prepared over. They are leaving with just paying for a soda? How about a quick salad or dessert? They cannot go away hungry; this is the worst thing you can do. I would offer a quick substitute at no charge to get them back. What did we do? We listened to his problem, respected his concerns, did not pre-judge. For the price of a beverage and a simple salad, they left happy.

#5: <u>Empower your employees.</u>

We would like to be there for every customer who is not happy, to make the time to resolve problems, and most importantly retain all potential customers. This will not always happen. We have to sleep, and take time to ourselves, so we may not always be there. That is why we need to have policies on how to handle situations, as well as empower our employees to listen and resolve problems. You will find that the problem that is resolved quickly is often forgotten. If we take a week or two to get back to someone then we made them feel that they and their problem were not that important.

When I was a Subway franchisee I empowered employees to make decisions, and we had guidelines to follow. If an employee was very busy and alone we told them to offer a free cookie to the person as they reached the register and to apologize for the wait. If the line was long they could offer a free drink to the people waiting until it was their turn. This often made a positive impression on a not so happy problem. Customers remember how they are treated, and when an employee goes that extra step it is impressionable.

Those 5%-ers . . . ever hear of them?

You know one, and you may have been one once. It is funny how you go into a place and an employee says, "Everyone is in a bad mood today." If we were to evaluate the experience we might find that there were actually one or two people who were unhappy, but since they were either more vocal or made you feel bad, you remembered them most. I used this to explain handling difficult people in previous workshops. As I explained to the people in attendance, "Yesterday I was in your business and there was a young man who came in and ordered such and such. He paid with exact change and left you a big tip. Do you remember him?" Most of the responses were no! I do this two or three times to a few different attendees. I then explain the point—these people come into your business every day! They actually make up most of your customer base, however they are what we could consider the normal people, and we do not memorize them. We are more likely to recall the cranky, oddly dressed, or rude person. So those people who stand out are those 5%-ers. We remember the 5%-ers, but not the normal or regular people we see all the time.

6: When You Have Missed an Opportunity

We all have had it happen! We had an employee who did not get us to resolve a problem, and now we have lost one of those valuable things we are trying so hard to get, and more importantly so hard to keep. (Customers!) A customer has come in and for one reason or another we have lost their interest in doing business with us. I know sometimes we feel like we are better off without them, but we cannot survive without them! Actually we need many more of them so we can do enough business that someday we may open more stores, start franchising, or even better yet, retire!

Here are some questions you may ask, and let me try to share the whys and what fors.

Should we care?

How do we respond?

When do we respond?

When do we not say anything?

Why should we bother? We will have other customers.

First of all, a customer has taken the time to point something out and we have a chance to learn from a situation. Let me remind you that a customer's perception is their reality! This is how they felt! If your policy is not going to answer their concerns, then they need to be informed. But, let me start by sharing some keys to handling complaints!

In the beginning of the book you learned why customers quit. Remember the different reasons that people leave? Well, here is the biggest category: attitude of indifference to the customer! This makes up 68% of the people that leave and never return. You are getting a second chance to address this issue because the customer has taken the time to share with you why they are unhappy. How you respond will determine if you let them leave or pull them back in.

Remember!

Up to 74% of your customers who complain will do business again if the situation is resolved! WE DO HAVE A CHANCE TO MAKE IT RIGHT!

Even more important, this number can go as high as 95% if we respond to the problem quickly! WE DO HAVE A CHANCE TO MAKE IT RIGHT!

So, here are some guidelines to remember when addressing complaints:

#1: <u>Do not judge the complainer prior to hearing them out</u>!

Your expression or demeanor may lose the opportunity. I often get people who call me over to say something nice about a staff member. If I walk out with a look of bother on my face, then they know I do not want to be bothered. I could turn this person away!

#2: <u>Listen!</u>

That is it! Just listen. Then repeat what you hear in order to make sure that you have it clear. Write down important details so you do not forget. Of all of the things I share this is one of the most important. Sometimes people just want to be heard. They see something that is not right, and they want to make you aware of it. It does not mean they want something for free! I recall having people tell me of slow service, or of food that was not hot enough. I listen and clarify. I offer a resolution, looking for their approval. This has now been resolved and quickly. I have made a SAVE!

In another situation, a customer asked me to come to his table and shared a problem. When he arrived at the register I had taken 25% off of his tab. He was a little upset to see that a discount was applied; he said he just wanted to let me know. I made him save face, I said, "Sir, this was because you took the time to bring an important issue to my attention. I cannot fix something that I don't see as broken. By your telling me that things were not okay I can address them with the staff. This is for your taking the time to share it with me." He was okay with it.

#3: <u>Act Quickly!</u>

We have got the call. This person wants to be heard. Take the time to listen, or send the best listener to the person who will share! This improves our chances to retain that customer. Then, when you get the information, address it quickly. A return call from the right person thanking them for the call and the opportunity will show that caller that they mattered. (Even if a reward has not been offered or called for.)

#4: <u>Be Sincere!</u>

This person or persons have taken the time to share their thoughts. Even if they are not feasible for your business, they are sharing. Thank them for their time, and share that you will keep it in your thoughts, or maybe for future development or a future staff meeting. Thank them! Your facial expression should show attention as they speak and that they have shared something of value. Even if it will not work for you, it is a suggestion from a paying customer!

#5: <u>Respond!</u>

As mentioned above, after you have listened to the customer and they have finished sharing, respond! Start by restating or clarifying what had happened. Thank them for taking the time to share, and how they will help you build in the future. If you pass them again as they leave, thank them again, and wish them a nice day. Make them feel like they helped.

#6: <u>Be prompt!</u>

When you are informed of a call or an in store customer wanting to see you, be prompt. If you have not noticed the customers watch moves much faster than a normal watch. What may have been 3 minutes in real time was 10 minutes on their watch and they feel unimportant. A caller probably will not wait that long for a manager.

Just yesterday we had a customer pick up a large order and they did not receive an item that was to be included. When this customer called the store to speak to the manager she was irate and why not? The manager who spoke to the customer offered to deliver the missed item and he was told no. She said she would call and speak to the manager in the morning. I was called to be informed of the problem. I was to be off the day she was going to call and wanted to make the most of this situation. I called my assistant who was opening in the morning, and shared what he was to expect. To prevent a nasty call, I jumped the situation by having the manager call the customer first thing in the morning. He called and told her that he was aware that an item was missed and wanted to see how he could correct it? The customer was not only pleasant, but she was amazed that we took the time to call her. This story just says be prompt!

UNHAPPY
CUSTOMER
TELLS

HAPPY
CUSTOMER
TELLS

IGNORE YOUR CUSTOMERS AND THEY WILL GO AWAY!

SO WILL:

SALES, REPEAT BUSINESS, TIPS, PROFITS

7. Idea Bank—Uh-Ohs Vs. Kudos

The following items are my observations that will show examples of how customers should and should not be treated. Sometimes as we read print we do not see it all too clearly. However, when someone says, "See that car? It is green!" then you see a green car. I will show examples of some great opportunities as well as some areas where someone had an opportunity and failed.

Each will be followed with a ***What Happened?*** and ***What Should Have Happened?***

I call this section "Uh-Ohs Vs. Kudos."

Uh – Ohs :

One day just after moving to our new neighborhood, we stopped at the local Sam's Club to pick up some items. We had been there a while, and as you know, that means we bought more items then we went for. We arrived at the first line and pulled up to pay. We had used one of their flatbed carts and the employee at the register said we had to go to the line next to him for flatbed checkout. We said, "There is no one over there and the sign says closed." He said, "Signs don't mean anything," and waved his hand as if to say, just move!

What Happened?

We the customers were made to look as though we were stupid! Now I have teenage kids, and I have teenage employees, so I knew what had happened. The manager of this store missed a training opportunity, and it could have been a costly one. I often refer to a process about why we do what we do. This process has to be done throughout our business in order for things to work. The manager or supervisor probably told this young employee that they had a new lane and all flatbed carts were to go there! The part he missed was why, and how to tell the guest.

What Should Have Happened?

The manager should have told the young employee that they reserved this extra lane for those with large purchases, and the lane was a little wider for the carts. When the customers need a cashier there please notify the supervisor. (This is what the store's general manager told us when we called to share our shocking experience!)

✹✹✹✹✹

This one comes to mind after I just wrote one on a super hairstylist. She earned my business and made me want to come back there each time I needed a haircut. Here is a new story though. We lived in a small town in Southwest Florida. We lived a block off of the main through road, so when it was time to get a haircut it was easy for me to walk two blocks to the place that I had visited for five years almost faithfully. The question is, Why? It is funny to say that when I needed a haircut, it was usually noticed by my wife first, and then it was an impulse decision. With time being of value, I usually chose the same place, just a short walk away. This place was usually the shortest wait, and I could get in and out in an hour or so. I share this "Uh-Oh" because I was a customer who visited this place usually every month for five years. I remember more about the people than they remembered me. I would request the manager, who was a little more attentive, but I was still never greeted or said hello to.

This was the time that I owned a Subway franchise, and I sent a lunch platter in to market the nearby store, and still was never recognized. I recall one stylist who liked to vacation on her own, she would take cruises and never went with anyone. Another one had a small child who was constantly ill, and had to miss a lot of work. This is one of my peeves and probably yours as well? I don't like to be taken care of by someone while they talk constantly to someone else. This happened often, if not always, in this store. The stylists spent more time speaking to each other about dating, kids, boyfriends, breaks, etc. than they did speaking to their clients. It was shame that no one saw this as part of the service. Remember when people used to ask you how you were doing, and made small talk that made you feel comfortable? They don't remember it here!

What Happened?

The stylist had as many as sixty opportunities to make a loyal customer a happy one, and failed miserably. They had a chance to make a few more dollars with each visit and they again failed.

What Should Have Happened?

As anyone who offers a service, they should focus on the person or persons that they are performing for at that time. It was good to see that they were outspoken people, but they needed to take that energy and capitalize on it by talking to the guest! In a private discussion with a hairstylist sometime later, I found that a common tip for a low-priced cut was $2 to $3. So a little extra attention would account for maybe a greater tip?

✻✻✻✻✻

We had been looking for a new place to eat and found a nice sandwich shop that had a different concept in it. So we gave it a try. It was good food, and the service was pretty quick, so we were sold. We had been in a few times, and the food was good! We were pleased to see that they were building a new location closer to our home, and we would have less of a distance to travel. But something was missing in the new store. Although they still had the eight to ten people working when we visited, they had slipped on some of the key training points with some of this staff. We walked in and went right to the area where it says "order here." There was a young lady standing at the register just staring at the television they had on in the store. We just waited; we figured a commercial would come on shortly and her attention would turn back towards the people that were going to help pay her salary that night. Well, we got impatient and just cleared our throats to let her know we were there. This was not a good thing. We got the death look, and were asked in a poor attitude, "What do you want?"

What Happened?

This was a new store that had opened just weeks before and these people were getting a chance to build a new customer base. I use the old saying, "You only get one chance to make that first impression." We had been users of the product before, so we knew the food was good. We just thought the service was below par. If we were making our first ever visit it would not have been one that would get us back in!

What Should Have Happened?

Training! Every employee in that store needed to know the goals of the company, and if there was a mission statement, what it was and how they were going to make it work. All employees needed to know what part they played, and what a customer really means to a business. We had a cute slogan printed on our paychecks so the employees got the message every week when they cashed their checks. The heading on the check said, "From the customers of Subway 1421." This is the store where they worked and it was payment from the people who made it happen! Customers! This needs to be a continual training that includes the process of "inspect what you expect." Make sure that employees are doing what we expect of them by inspecting what they are doing.

Extra Note!

In other parts of this book I mention where we need to monitor what and how we are doing. In this line of work we can measure a lot of areas of our business to see how we are doing, and we can get better. We can time the rate of service to see if we get them in and through quick enough for those in a hurry. But, in this case we need to measure the quality of service. We can offer a comment card to be filled for review. We can offer a Web site to go to and make comments, or just ask, "How did we do today?"

In one of my stores we added a hotline number on the front of the door, and we let the employees know that we were getting feedback. We would reward a positive comment and also share areas where we needed to grow!

*****

Part of my book writing took place during the regrouping after Hurricane Charley. This was a major storm that hit Southwest Florida. During this aftermath we met a lot of good people doing more than their share, and we met people like those in the next two stories, who took advantage of people who were already having it hard!

Example A) I was commuting from a distance away for work, and this area had little to no damage. I stopped each morning to get some supplies, food, etc., and tried to help some of our managers and employees through their tough times. I found a station that was open, and had gas. I stopped there each day to stock up on my way to the damaged areas. We all have heard stories of price gouging during tough times. What these business owners call supply and demand some call taking advantage of those people who are desperately in need. On two consecutive days I stopped and bought the same exact items, and on the second day I found that I was being charged $6 more for the same few items.

What Happened?

This was a business that had a captive audience that could have been made faithful consumers if the owner had been compassionate, understanding, or just honest! He may have had people that may not otherwise come into his business. Because he had what others could not offer he took advantage of the customers coming in.

What Should Have Happened?

He should have been true to his business. He needed to see opportunity in getting people to come in, and more importantly come back. He failed! Needless to say I did not stop again, and we would drive an extra exit for anything we needed.

*****

Example B) In another station there were a few branded concepts that were doing business. We knew about the famous doughnut place and thought this would be a quick pick-up item, and without power a few people would love a hot cup of coffee. We included this in our trip to this station. We were waiting in a small line to get some things and we were behind a lady and her daughter. They spoke of their sorrows and how they would have to have the little girl go stay with a relative while mom got things fixed. This was sad, but the next part is even worse. As they reached the counter they got their few items. The lady at the counter handed them their change and she slid the tip cup towards the woman. The lady just smiled and walked away. The lady at the register said to her coworker, "Some people are just cheap!" Hello! This is a woman sending her child away so she can live normally while she tries to get her life together!

What Happened?

These two ladies, although they had been there for at least a year, had no understanding of what a customer means to a business. It was a shame that these employees were not aware that some people have bigger problems than they did.

What Should Have Happened?

If anyone heard what this woman said, they would boycott this station and never offer them any business. If this was said during harsh times, I wonder what they say when times are okay and a consumer does not tip? Instead of judging they should have compassion.

Extra Note!

Earlier in this book I shared about judging people. A tipped employee can make their biggest mistake by prejudging someone. I had a server who not only did this, but she also spent more time looking to see what others were getting tipped by a customer who had tipped her poorly. She didn't ever consider it was the service, not the person. When she decided to leave I never gave it a second thought. I had lowered her shifts and she moved on. I would not have asked her back knowing these poor habits.

*****

I almost forgot a story of a situation that happened at a famous theme park. I had little ones at the time, and they were interested in visiting a new park that had just opened. As we were walking through the park on a very hot day we decided to stop for a beverage. As we approached one of the little roadside stands we walked in on an argument of two employees over a date the night before. We waited for our interruption to be a hint, to no avail. We left and went on to another food area.

What Happened?

Perception is reality! We wanted a drink and left without satisfying our reason for being there. "We went to another food place, but since we were still inside the theme park the company ultimately didn't suffer. We were captive customers."? We were disappointed and we, like others, will tell others!

What Should Have Happened?

Everyone in business needs to remember the following: Hire the best person for the job, and train, train, train! This particular theme park is the leader in their area of hiring and training. I wrote a great story of other visits to this park and why they are a leader in their group! We just happened along to experience the one person who was either a poor catch or did not respond well to the training provided. We are constantly looking for good people, and when we let them know what we expect, we on occasion will get someone who slips through the cracks. This is what happened here. Our goal is to eliminate those who do not continue to follow the map we provide.

*****

This one happened in front of my own eyes. The place I am currently at has the servers seating the customers as they enter the restaurant. In this situation two employees were getting a drink and talking in the service area, when there was a small wait at the door. The customers asked if they should seat themselves and the employee barked out, "NO!"

What Happened?

Ouch! We have a training opportunity and in a big way! This is what this book is really about. We get these opportunities to see things that we would not appreciate, and know that our customers do not appreciate, and we get a chance to fix them. If we are constantly looking at how we are doing then we can see things that may need fixing.

But, how do we respond? Do we talk to the two employees and let them know what happened and why? Or do we walk away? This is why customers quit!

Instead of "What Should Have Happened," How About "What Did I Do?"

I sent for these two servers, and as they entered my office they said, "We have things to do," and I said, "Did you when the customers were waiting at the door?" I shared that two things happened out there. They missed the waiting customers, and left them standing, and when the customer questioned the wait they yelled at him, instead of apologizing. I shared my favorite saying in this field, "A customer's perception is their reality!" If you ask any employee who has been with me what my most famous saying is, they will share this. Why? Because I always tell them what was wrong, why it was wrong, and why we are making the change to fix it! They were instructed on what to do in the future and how to handle the situation better next time. The one young employee who was involved made her mind up to go visit those people and apologize for not getting to them sooner. (She got it!) The other employee left a few weeks later!

*****

Here is another in-house story that turned into a learning opportunity. I have a cashier who means the world to me, and she would do just about anything for me. She has been working longer than I have been living and probably has experienced it all. One day a lady came to the register to pay their bill and they had a travelers' check. They had endorsed the second signature block as they were waiting to pay. She chose to let them know that they were not to sign it unless it was in front of her. Instead of being the customers these people were now kids being yelled at by a parent, or students at the principal's office. I was not able to witness this myself but was told by an employee.

What Happened?

A customer who was just visiting to patronize my business has now been embarrassed by an employee. People want to go where they are welcome, and do not return to a place where they are not treated well.

What Should Have Happened?

A simple solution would have been for the employee to ask for an ID as proof. She could have asked by saying, "Excuse me, may I please see your ID? These were endorsed before you arrived, so I just need to verify them." Most importantly, she should remember to say, "Thank you." No harm, no foul!

Extra Note!

We have changed our procedures over the years, but what I like best is when an employee hands the customer's credit card back they thank them by the name on the credit card. "Thank You, Mr. Long, have a great night!" Is a great send-off to a great experience.

$$*****$$

I went into a restaurant at closing one night to pick up an employee and saw an experience that made me feel bad for the customers. Since this was not my location I was not able to resolve it.

I walked in the door and was waiting near their podium where customers are greeted and seated. A small family walked in the door and was met by an employee. This employee had a chance to say hello and welcome, but instead chose to tell the customers that they just made it in. She said they were actually closed, but the manager was not there to lock the doors yet! This started badly and got worse. Another employee went to the podium and said, "Don't seat them with me, I am leaving soon," at which point the first employee said, "I am not taking them." How do these people feel? Unwanted?

What Happened?

A customer who had a choice decided to give this restaurant some of his hard-earned money. They had a chance to make him a faithful user of their products, and instead made him to feel that he and his family were an inconvenience. They may leave and say next time we should come earlier, but realistically the service remained poor and this restaurant lost a customer who will never return. In the customer's eyes they will make a better choice next time!

What Should Have Happened?

A manager needs to be visible and be aware of how things are done at closing. As I am in the same restaurant chain I know that out of sight is out of mind! The real problem is this can not be taught to an employee. An employee who has this attitude towards a customer is in the wrong business, and needs to be a casualty!

Extra Note!

I am constantly evaluating my staff and looking to see who has a generally good attitude. When someone is moody, or always grumpy, they cannot offer great service. We refer to these employees as poison, and they need to be moved on before they infect the others!

In all of my years in business, I have held a level of expectation and no matter what it was, my employees were expected to perform at that level. When they succeeded, the results were positive for all. But, the key was, we always performed at that level. This will be true in your business as well. The real question will be, "How high is the bar?"

*****

In my travels with Subway I had the opportunity to do some small group workshops on customer service. This was one of my first experiences at public speaking, and after this challenge I encountered I realized that I really liked it.

I was in the Fort Myers area, and I met with a small group of franchisees. I noticed in one person's store they charged customers for what they offered as free toppings. As I was speaking he asked a question that I thought was meant to stump me. His question was, "Let's say that you have a woman who comes into your store every single day and she asks for extra olives on her sandwich? What do you do?" I thought if I repeated the question I would better understand where there would be a problem with this. "So let me make sure I got this right. This person comes into your business every day for lunch and buys a sandwich? She always asks for extra olives on her sandwich?" He said, "Yep! Sometimes as many as twenty." It hit me! I said, "Let me make sure that I have this right. This person comes into your store every day? And buys a sandwich? And she asks for extra olives?" He said, "Yep!" I am starting to enjoy this. After repeating this one more time, emphasizing on the "comes in every day and she buys a sandwich," the others in the group got it, and started to acknowledge. But, he did not, so I had to give him the answer. I said, "Tony, I would start by asking her what her name was. I have a faithful customer and I need to know her by name. Then I would count out twenty olives every day and have them ready for Mary. I then would hope that Mary would bring a friend for lunch since we treated her so well! Do you get it?"

At Subway we worried about the expensive topping. Olives! We also were taught that for everyone who wanted a little more there were probably five or six who did not ask for any!

✳✳✳✳✳

I had been faithful to a brand, and as I traveled I found myself stopping at their drive-thru for a quick bite. In those years this giant was a leader in many categories. But, this fell off quickly. During my time as a chairman on a local marketing board for Subway, I was often given a list that advertising gurus use to judge their clients and how they rank amongst their competition. One category that the giant did not lead in was the order accuracy. They made attempts to fix this, however they did not seem to be too sincere.

In multiple visits to stores I would ask for my burger to not have onions. When I would drive away from the window the burger had onions. Did I wait in line again or go inside? Often it was neither. I would eat the French fries and throw the rest out. In the years to come they added a sticker: "This order was double-checked for accuracy." They told you they were checking, but guess what, they weren't. Orders were still wrong, and we now had an added sticker that held our receipts on. They took another step recently. Now they have a sign at the window that says "Please check your order before leaving." Now it is your job to check for accuracy. If you didn't catch it, is it your fault?

What Happened?

We again had someone who chose us, and we disappointed them. We hired people that were either careless or they did not get trained properly to complete a very important task. If these employees had someone explain to them at hiring why it should be important, they would be more likely to complete the task!

What Should Have Happened?

Proper hiring and training! Hire people with good attitudes and train the skill! Have signs on the inside reminding employees of their duties. It is their duty to be accurate. Inspect what you expect! Survey your customers. Maybe a slip in the bag that asks for feedback and a small reward for returning it to the manager. A free drink?

Extra Note!

In my restaurant I have a drive-thru. Our meals are a little more extensive and have a little more assembly required by the attendant. When we get calls of a wrong or missing item we usually replace it, with an apology. I started a new system soon after I came to this restaurant and have watched the problem get smaller by execution. This is what we did; we held a meeting and showed that we had a full sheet of over thirty entries in one month of unhappy customers who called about missing or incorrect orders. We told the employees that the results of an unhappy customer is a lost customer. I needed their help to be more accurate. I made a sign for over the drive-thru that says "Accuracy please!" We made a contest that would result in a drawing in sixty days for anyone who's name did not make the list. In a recent meeting I reviewed that we still had some issues, however our list took four months to fill up! Great job! Then we had a drawing for gift cards!

*****

This is something that I find a little offensive. After eating dinner at a restaurant, Like a lot of places, the server here completes the sale by bringing the check and carrying their own bank; they make the change. On this particular occasion I went to this restaurant and at the end of the meal I was brought the check. It was for $36. I handed the server the check back with a $100 bill. The server looked at it and asked that awful question; "Do you need change?" Is this a silly question? How often do you eat out and tip a server 177%?

What Happened?

A customer was put into an uncomfortable situation. Any time we put a customer at risk they fall into that 68% category where people leave due to employee indifference.

What Should Have Happened?

I have heard employees use a reply that is not offensive and I wonder why everyone is not taught to use a common response? I think it should be a statement that would not offend, where the employee just says, "I will be right back with your change." If the customer intended for you to keep the balance they will tell you and there will be an opportunity to thank them. This response should be the same for everyone who is cashing out.

Extra Note!

We have to treat customers like we would treat guests in our home. I would say that all of us would want to make our guests feel at ease.

*****

Here is a similar story with the same point. I had a manager who was hired for his computer skills and hard work ethic, and we thought we could teach him the rest. We had small things that would come up, but they were often learning situations that we could use to explain to him the customer's perception. (There is that saying again!)

We have an all-you-can-eat plan on a few items. This manager was working in the kitchen, and like all managers do, he was checking tickets for accuracy, and to account for all items served. When he saw that a certain person had reordered several times he made the comment to the server, "What, more ribs? I would like to see the person who could eat all of those ribs!" I was on the outside of the kitchen at the register and heard the comment. I had a few customers who were paying, and they too heard the comment. I had to overreact the situation back at the manager to show this was not acceptable, and more importantly, not tolerated.

What Happened?

As I mentioned in the example above, we have a situation where customers are not comfortable, and they do not like to return where they are not comfortable. In this case the uncomfortable customer did not have to be the person that was being talked about, it could have been anyone who could hear.

What Should Have Happened?

All employees have to be aware of what should be said and when. If it is not something they would say themselves to a guest in their home, then why say it recklessly when someone could hear it?

Extra Note!

When I took over this restaurant I observed for two or three weeks before implementing major changes. One of the best things I did was set a rule of thumb for all servers, cooks, and managers. First, let me share that the layout of this restaurant is so the food pick-up window is at the front by the register, and the cooks are in view of the front. I passed a rule that is still shared to every new employee early in their training process. No negative talking will be tolerated at the window, going either direction. If a server needs to replace an item that was either not what the customer had ordered, or not hot enough, it is always brought to the back of the house to be addressed. This is so we do not have an accident like with this manager. We do not have a cook getting defensive, we do not have a server who talks badly about a customer, and in our customer's eyes we keep a sincere interest.

This is just a chance to prevent an issue. This rule does go both ways; cooks cannot talk to servers negatively or in high tones , and servers cannot show anger or problems either!

We recently stayed at a large hotel on vacation in the famous Las Vegas. We had made reservations at a restaurant and had tickets for a show to follow. We had a pretty good plan with a little built-in time for error. We exited the hotel at the same area that we had arrived. As we walked out the doors a cab was unloading. We walked over to get into the cab, when a bellman stopped us from getting in. He said that this area was only for drop-off and we had to go to the other side of the hotel to catch a cab. I mentioned that we were in a little bit of a hurry, and he responded that there were cameras watching and we would have to go to the correct area. At this point two members of our group were already in this cab. We exited the cab and walked through the hotel to the other side. We got into a small line and started to wait. We were about the fourth group back so it should not have been that long. I am always looking at how things are done, and always wondering why things happened, so I did not miss what was happening. A bellman walked out the door with two guests and a few bags. They were ushered to the front of the line and given the next cab to arrive. This happened not once but three times. The following day we went to the correct side of the hotel to catch a cab and again had a small wait. Again, we were second in priority to those people coming out with bags.

What Happened?

Several times in this book I share the phrase "perception is reality." This is the case here. I shared with my wife, the bell captain, and later the supervisor, that it appeared that those people who had luggage were given priority because they were tipping. It may not have been the case, but this is how it looked to me. I asked the bell captain as I got to the front of the line why those people were getting their cabs first. I asked if it was because they tipped. And he said, "No! This is policy." I shared my story from the night before and he said that they always rush people through that are in a hurry. Yet me and my guests were taken out of our cab! I later spoke to a supervisor, who said this was not a policy, and it would be addressed.

What Should Have Happened?

When working for tips we are all encouraged to go that extra yard to make the tipping person more appreciative. Yet we have to keep in mind that if we turn off a potential tipper we are losing money in the long run! In the beginning we should have been given a reason why we could not board the cab there. Then we should have been permitted to ride since we were there.

Extra Note! ~

I like to share numbers and often have to use them on a big scale to get people's attention. I had a server meeting following a few bad comment cards. We spoke about why some of the things happened, customer perception, and also the numbers.

Here is how it went:

Last week we waited on 4,286 customers.

It worked out to be 2,000 parties of various numbers.

We used 101 server shifts, so you each had 20 parties on average per shift.

Let's say that each day one of you disappointed a customer who left, never to return.

In three months we would have lost 90 parties or one opportunity for you to be sat! The rotation would be fewer when there are fewer guest to take care of. In the restaurant's eyes we would have lost 90 groups or 180 people. At $10.50 a ticket average we lose $98,280 in lost sales.

In the servers' eyes they lose one seating per shift. Eight shifts at $5 per seating equals $40 per week or $2,080 per year.

✵✵✵✵✵

I just bragged about a lunch at famous seafood restaurant and how the new server treated us like friends. We had a visit a few months back at a sister company that did not go nearly as well! This person was not introduced as a new server, but she showed that she was either very new or she was poorly trained. Some of the examples in this story will not be items that can be taught, but we do need to be out there looking and listening in the attempt to prevent them from happening.

We arrived and were greeted by a friendly young lady who was pregnant. She had a glow about her and welcomed us to the restaurant. We were ushered to a vacant table, and awaited our server. There was a server in the area who had flown by on two or three occasions with no acknowledgement. We must have looked little impatient because on her fourth trip by she yelled out, "I'll be back!" What a greeting! We continued to wait for a few minutes and she returned. We are regulars here as well, so we always order the same items. When she brought the soups and salads she had to notice that all of the drinks were empty. After a few minutes she returned with our dinners. I am not sure who is responsible for spacing the courses, but they did not. We were encouraged to push the soup aside so she could place the entrees on the table. At this point the drinks were still empty! After a few bites of my meal (which was consistent, great as always!) I went to the bar to refill my soda. I asked the bartender if we were to come to the bar for refills? I was hoping he would let someone know that there was a problem brewing? My wife and daughter don't like attention so they left theirs empty.

What Happened?

A poor start preceded a poor visit. We gave the bartender a chance to see a problem and seek help, but it was not picked up on. There are more people who would not give an opportunity for improvement, they would just quit! We tried to get help, and tried to have someone resolve the issue.

What Should Have Happened?

When training we need to have an outline of the steps to great service. We need to train this and make sure that the servers know this before they are sent out on their own. Scary thought, this server had a unique hairstyle with multiple colors in it. We have seen this person on several occasions. This person has made an impact on many customers.

The bartender! Usually an observant type since their clientele sit apart and need to have someone keep an eye on them, the bartender here missed this. He should have notified a manager that a customer had to come to the bar and get refills, so the manager could have looked in on the server. She may need help; the situation could have been saved.

Extra Note!

I am not the person who wants something for nothing. I will often wait until I leave the restaurant to share with a manager or their team about an incident. As I was leaving I asked for the manager's card and the young lady said, "Yes, if you could wait for just a moment I can get him for you." It was in the middle of lunch so I instead sent a letter. I always send it anonymous so they do not feel the pressure of having to respond. The exception is if it is a call to inform of theft or a necessary caution, in which case I will call immediately!

*****

The cardinal sin a restaurant can commit is to ignore their customers. There is a saying, "Ignore your customers and they will go away!" This applies not just when they arrive but when they are ready to leave. We went into a new restaurant in town. They probably do not know how tough they have it. They are located in a mall and the rents in malls are much higher than any other location I have checked into. Their break-even point is much higher than you could imagine. This same restaurant has placed full-colored ads in the Sunday paper with specials for the past fifteen weeks. After seeing their ads we thought we would check them out. We went up to the hostess stand and asked for a table for three. There was no wait, so we went right in. We sat down and waited for the server. Everyone was running around, and one server passed us on three occasions not even acknowledging us. A young man came by and asked for our drink order and then left. We waited a good ten more minutes and he did not return. Where'd he go? What happened? We ended up leaving, and we went across the hall to another restaurant.

What Happened?

When the manager/owner saw that sales were low he spent thousands of dollars to get more people to be aware of the restaurant and get them to stop in. We call this ATU. First you make them *aware* of your business, then you solicit them to come in and *try* your product (or services), and then if you do a great job you may get them to come back and become *users* of your products.

This employee was not given a guide as to how long a customer can sit without recognition, and again until their drinks are at the table, and how long the food should take. If there is a plan it is easier to teach and also easier to follow. There was a lot of money spent to get people in, and therefore a lot of money that was being wasted.

<u>What Should Have Happened?</u>

Whoever trained these employees needed to have an outline of the steps to great service. We need to train this and make sure that the servers know this before they are sent out on their own. This employee needed to have some assistance, and a manager needs to be available to see and resolve any issues.

<u>Extra Note!</u>

Training goes hand in hand with explaining. All employees need to be informed of what is happening in the restaurant. Pre-shift meetings and other regular meetings will let them know what the managers are trying to accomplish, and what role they play. You need their participation to make this work! This is a great time to have a contest! Employee contests with rewards will make them take instant ownership. As they share in Sonny's BBQ everyone is a stakeholder in the company. Everyone has something to gain, but more importantly something to lose!

If you would like more information on ATU and the secret of local marketing, please visit our Web site and look at the Fun Shops on *Am I Fishing in the Right Pond?*

KUDOS :

This one goes out to the famous steakhouse with the Australian theme. My wife and I were eating at a restaurant and sat next to a table where the customer was telling a friend about a wonderful experience that is worth repeating! She had been at an Outback Steakhouse where she had asked for something not on the menu and the employee followed up with the manager. The manager had replied, "Sure, that would be no problem!" The young lady who was getting this positive feedback smiled as she remembered the manager's words (even though I had my back turned to her, I could feel it! We all like to hear the good every now and then!) The manager said, "It is our policy if we can do it, do it! Hence the slogan 'No Rules Just Right!'_"

What Happened?

Another satisfied customer! And this customer became what I like to refer to as a roaming billboard for their business! This woman was so happy she followed the rule of thumb and told others! We were nearby so we had the chance to hear this great story. Guess where we ate the next time we were out?

What Should Have Happened?

Exactly that!

Extra Note!

I share in my training workshops that we all need to train employees, but we also need to empower them as well to make some of the small decisions that will better our business. This has happened here. The management staff was trained that there are no rules, just make it right!

KUDOS—OUTBACK STEAKHOUSE!

******

This one is a true kudos for a hairstylist who knows why she is there to do her job! After visiting a few different salons in the new area we had just moved to, I had the opportunity to experience someone who knows how to perform and someone else who did not. I walked in and was greeted with a smile by Laura. She was quick to say that someone would be right with me. After a short wait, Laura was the one who was going to cut my hair. I enjoyed a little small talk while she cut my hair. On a return visit (yes, she earned my business a second time), I walked in and was told that it would be an hour before she would have an open appointment. Imagine that she had a following as well! I agreed to wait and take my turn. When I arrived back she smiled and thanked me for waiting. I was first reminded how I got my hair cut last time, and asked if we were doing the same at this time? Again, we had some small talk but this was a little different. The hairstylist next to her was huffing and puffing each time she spoke, as if she was being bothered. All I wanted was a good haircut and someone to focus on me. Laura understands this part, and as long I lived in that area she was the one to cut my hair.

What Happened?

Another satisfied customer! This person (Laura) has learned it is the money she is tipped that makes up her true income. I am not sure, but she seemed to be impressed by the $5 tip I left each time on a $10 haircut. She always smiled and greeted me when I arrived. The salon had a customer who was faithful to their shop because of the product they had (Laura).

What Should Have Happened?

Exactly that!

KUDOS — FIRST CHOICE HAIR CUTTERS! AND LAURA! FINE JOB!

✶✶✶✶✶

This is our "What About Mary?" story! We had the opportunity to become regulars at a wing joint in Fort Lauderdale. We had a friend tell us about it once, and we became quite regular (two to three times a week). How did this happen? Well, we met Mary. Mary was a server who worked at this place and was really great at what she did! She would remember what we ate, drank, and always offered a smile and some humor! Now this may sound like a story you all have had, but it goes a lot further than this. We had been through a few rough parts over the year. Mary, being the complete server and having been empowered, often fixed problems without any hesitation. We had a long wait one visit and she went back and checked on our food. On another visit a foreign object was found in our food; she apologized and quickly replaced the food. She was always quick to respond, and very sincere. Mary moved on from this wing place and ended up at an Outback. We went to see Mary one night with a large group of people. Mary had not missed a beat. She was very attentive, and made us feel very special with the people we brought. It made us feel like this was our place, and we had a friend here. Mary was special and knew how to take care of her guests so they would take care of her!

What Happened?

Another satisfied customer! It is not known how long Mary has been a server, but it is apparent that she is aware of what people are looking for. She remembers people, and what they want when she is taking care of them.

What Should Have Happened?

Exactly that! We all have businesses that have people taking care of our clients, customers, or patrons. If we have more Mary's then we can count on our true image being shown!

Extra Note!

I attended a seminar recently for Sonny's franchisees. In this workshop we spoke of different items that the company had planned to do, and in addition they talked of changing their focus. The term "stakeholders" was introduced and can be a great way to see your employees. They are true stakeholders in your company and can be those that make a positive investment, like Mary!

KUDOS —OUR MARY! ONE OF THE BEST!

*****

This is a winning holiday story! How would you like to be the only grocery store that was open on Christmas Day? Or the manager who had to be on duty that morning? Well, this Christmas morning, like many others, we realized we had forgotten some items, and also saw that we never had enough batteries. We went into this store and were greeted by someone who was smiling and was greeting everyone as they entered. She wished them great holiday wishes, and also safe and happy New Years. She was working at a register, either because she was allowing others to have this day off, or she was working there because someone had taken the day off. We met this woman as we entered the store, and saw her again as we left. Her spirits remained very high throughout the visit, but it went one step further. As we passed the deli, bakery, and clerks in this store, we noticed that their spirits were the same! Everyone was okay with being at work, and showed it with their pleasant attitudes.

What Happened?

Another satisfied customer! This was a day when no one wanted to be out, and more importantly no one wanted to be at work. This was an experience that was memorable. We were faithful to our grocery store, but they were closed on this day. We gave the competition a chance and they have won us over!

What Should Have Happened?

Exactly that!

Extra Note!

You will have things that you will need to have your employees do that will not appear to be favorable to them. The negative talk will kill the morale. We can overcome this by having a meeting to explain the problem, and discuss options for a cure. Including employees in the problem and solution sells a decision that they took part in. Keep in mind that all of the upper management has to be sold for this to work. If they start the negative talk then the idea will never make it through the staff. In this case they probably asked for volunteers who may not have plans, and offered rewards to those who worked. Some people have family out of the area so they just assume they will work a little overtime, rather than be home alone.

Kudos—Albertson's and their management team!

*****

I am trying to jump back and forth with the "Kudos" and "Uh-Ohs" to keep my spirits up! I just wrote about the two horror stories of Hurricane Charley. Here is the most memorable story about the hurricane:

At this same exit where the doughnut shop and the convenience store are, there is a famous burger place. On our first trip back to the damaged area I stopped here to get something to eat. I walked in the front lobby where a young man was mopping, and he gave me a smile, and said, "How are you today?" I was in such shock that my chin must have hit the floor! When I reached the counter a young lady gave me a smile and said, "Hi there! What can I get for you today?" The visit finished with the young lady and the young man saying good-bye. I am not sure if I looked as though I was on tough times, but I left feeling like a million bucks. I even went out to my car, parked, and took the time to write this down. I wanted to tell everyone how I felt this day. I promise that I told no fewer than six people that day.

What Happened?

Either I met the two nicest kids on earth, or someone took the time to have a team meeting and say, "Guys, we are going to be busy today. There are not too many places open, and we will be busy. Today, there will be a lot of unhappy people, and people who may appear angry! We need to be a little more patient today and show a lot of compassion."

What Should have Happened?

Exactly that!

I saw what appeared to be the owner in this store as I visited. She was quite busy and I decided to call back. I never did make communications, but I do have them on my list of people who will get a copy of this book.

Extra Note!

This reminded me of the old saying, "Kill them with kindness!" This was a slaying. These are great kids who have been given great direction. The credit in this story goes to the person who actually hired these two young people. This store and the person who does the hiring got the right people!

Kudos—McDonald's @ Jacaranda, and staff!

*****

We were visiting Mickey Mouse's home, and having a memorable visit, when we noticed that one of the kids misplaced the camera after taking a picture. We know that recovering lost items is a hit or miss chance. But, it was the person who comforted us during this dilemma who made the experience a memorable one. We went back to the raft ride and over to the island and the young lady who was the captain asked if we were going back over. We explained that we had lost our camera and we were going over to look for it. From her expressions of remorse to her direction on getting a disposable for the rest of the visit, to the final stop of checking in lost and found at the end of the day to see if it was returned, her help was priceless and very sincere. She cared for our loss and made the effort to help us with recovery.

What Happened?

Someone hired an employee who enjoys her job, and likes to go to work each day. This is what we call in the working world as a find. And a great one at that! You have to hire the right attitude and then teach the skill. Well, in this case they did. Nicole saw a problem and directed us on how we can continue to enjoy our visit despite our lost item.

What Should Have Happened?

This is not something you teach, it is a great result of a person who was sought out and found to fill an important position. As the old saying says, "Hire the attitude and train the skill."

Extra Note!

In the back of this book I reference other projects. *Did I Get the Right Person to Play this Part?"* explains the key elements of recruiting and hiring people to fill the important positions that we are all looking to fill. Remember that your employees usually are the ones who take care of your most important commodity—your customers!

Kudos—Nicole and Walt Disney World Orlando!

*****

Some companies are trying daily to overcome reputations of poor service when they rely so much on phone conversations. This is a cute story of the friendliest computerized phone service I have ever heard. We had just got hit by a lightning storm and our phone was knocked out. We have spoken to customer service reps for this company before and we always seem to get great service fast. We now had a day that they were closed and we had to talk to a machine. They tried to troubleshoot the problems with a series of questions. The responses told me that this company was going one more step towards customer satisfaction. One of the first questions was, "Do you have a dial tone?" My wife said no, and the response was, "I am sorry, we will look right into that!"

What Happened?

A company probably got feed back on how the customers were perceiving there phone service, and acted on the input received? A level of customer service was raised to meet customer expectations even when it is not a live person.

What Should Have Happened?

Exactly that!

This is unique because they may be ahead of a trend to come. A lot of us feel that in some areas we have no choice who the provider will be and we have to put up with the service level, no matter how poor. This company understands what the customers mean to their company, and strives for perfection.

KUDOS—VERIZON SERVICES!

✶✶✶✶✶

When I arrived at Sonny's I had some newer and less experienced servers who felt that they had no chance to make money because existing servers had a lot of regulars. This was a real difficult one to get them to understand. However, if you have people who ask for a particular server every time they come in, there either has to be something given away, or really good service.

Or, maybe people do not like change? Imagine if you went to the same place for lunch every Friday, and when Lu waited on you, she not only said hi to you at the door, but she brought your favorite sweet tea just the way you like it, and she knew what you wanted as well as you did. How would this make you feel? *Special?* This is why you come in and ask for Lu! Just a special note, when Lu left, she had a harder task to fill. She had to hand several batons over to servers who would maintain her level of service!

There was one individual who I watched, and on the second shift of keeping my eye on him, I found out why he had the request. It was not because he was our only male server at the time, or the fact that he looked like a real ladies' man. I was seating the customers who came in the door and a couple with a small child asked for Steve. I brought them to his table and he walked up behind me with their drinks in hand. This is a little something that makes people remember you versus the competition. Yes, when you are a server and you work among others, you have a small competition.

Then there is this one server who gets a lot of the larger groups, and also the adults who like the mature person who does not play or get distracted when they are doing their work. This server never has to be asked twice, and always remembers a face. Again, that little something extra is what gets them back to you!

There is one more special person that I give all my credit of hard work and dedication to. As I was growing up, I had a mom who worked so hard. She always had at least two jobs, and she raised seven kids! This was a job in itself. I always refer to my mom when I want to share an example of a hard worker to my employees. I saw my mom as a professional server who was always giving and getting a little more. I remember seeing her walk out of the server areas with what seemed to be twenty drinks in her hands, a stack of plates, and a handful of napkins. She always knew what people needed before they did. She always had twice the station of others, and just worked really hard! There was no one better!

Kudos—Lu, Steven, Rosemary, and MOM!

*****

What a great lunch today. As I am trying to apply as much effort as I can to finish assembling my data, I am now given a great opportunity to add this story. We arrived at this famous seafood restaurant where we are accustomed to getting above-average service, and the hostess said, "I am seating you in a new station with a new server." Our first thought was, "Great, we have to break in a new one!" Well, this young man, Eric, really did a great job today. We arrived and were asked if we knew the specials and would we like to start with a beverage. He didn't stop there! He asked us if we wanted specific items, by name. This is more appealing, and gets your attention! He quickly returned and took our order. I believe this was one of the best visits to this restaurant that we have had, and we've had more than our share! We did not need to ask for refills on bread or drinks, or wait long for anything. If he was new, he was trained very, very well.

What Happened?

Another satisfied customer! This was a long day and we wanted a place that we enjoy on a regular basis to take care of us in the way we would expect. We were given a newer server who answered the calling. He was very nice, very attentive, and great at his job!

What Should Have Happened?

Exactly that! I mentioned that we wanted a place where we visit that they give us the service we are accustomed to, and we are regulars! This means they have earned our business on numerous occasions.

Extra Note!

Every business needs those regulars! In the world of tipped employees there are those people who come in and ask for the person who remembers them and gives them the attention that they deserve. If we could build that base alone we would have walking billboards everywhere!

KUDOS—A SPECIAL KUDOS TO ERIC AND THE STAFF AT RED LOBSTER!

*****

WOW! This is a big shocker, and I could not wait to get home to talk about it. I just got finished telling this same story in an email to Taco Bell's corporate Web site. I had just left work and my daughter had asked me to get something for her on my way home. I stopped by the local Taco Bell, and after at least a few not so pleasant trips I was amazed at this trip tonight. As I was getting off of the main road I saw a small line of cars and thought I could be there a while. When I got to the drive-thru road the line was moving quickly. I arrived at the speaker and the young person took my order and repeated it. As I approached the window I could see that this person was not only working hard, but she was so efficient in her work. As I arrived at the window she was very polite, and reminded me of the kind of person I would want to take care of my guests! I took the time to email Taco Bell about this person and how much she meant to their business.

What Happened?

Another satisfied customer! This is quick-service food service. Probably one of the hardest places to recruit staffing. Who wants to work fast food? Well, Loren does, and she is great at her job!

What Should Have Happened?

Exactly that! This may be the food of kids and teenagers, but they need parents to take them there to eat it. If you want me to take them to a place I will tolerate, then make it presentable, and take care of me!

Extra Note!

In my email to Taco Bell's corporate headquarters, I made a strong recommendation to have someone from the corporate office call her and share this great thing. In a survey I read a few years back they ranked things that employees wanted in a job. I know you are thinking pay topped the list? Actually, it was recognition that employees wanted. Someone to say thank you! Or nice job! My wife and I had a lot of employees over the years, and we always enjoyed having contests or giving recognition to good employees. We found a book, *1001 Ways to Reward Employees* by Bob Nelson. If you are a manager or employer you need this book. You need to know how to keep that great employee. Like Loren!

Kudos—Loren and the recruiter who hired her at the Taco Bell in Port Charlotte, Florida !

8. Consider the Numbers

Just some numbers to be aware of. If these numbers do not apply to your particular business, then take the average cost of items sold in your business, and calculate the losses if an employee loses a valued customer. Now do this again if that person tells ten more people, and if they tell ten *more* . . .

If:

You own or manage a grocery store chain, you have shoppers who are faithful to their favorite store that carries the freshest produce, and has the friendliest cashiers. One day one of your employees has a bad day and you lose a customer. If this customer spends $150 a week like we do in our trip to the grocery store, then you can lose $7,800 in business. Grocery stores have a lot of employees. What if four or five of them each lose a customer? This number grows rapidly. You must market to get people into your business versus your competition. You have to fight to get more customers, and then you have to replace those you have lost.

If:

You own or manage a salon and you have stylists who are turning away your valuable customers, then you have losses as well. A person who likes to go to the same place will be lost and you will lose them twelve times for this year. If you charge $12 for a haircut, then this person now has taken $144 in business with them. This does not include this person being an adult with two kids. He used to bring them with him, and they are now going to a new place.

Marketing usually involves a discount of the product, and then a great service has to happen for a customer to become faithful to your business. This was an investment that did not work.

Explain it to the hairstylist. "You do ten haircuts per shift and get $3 tip per cut? This is $30 a day. If we lose x number of customers then next month you will get eight cuts per shift or $24. This is a $6 loss per day; in 51 weeks of five days each you will lose $1,530 in tips as well!"

If:

You own or manage a restaurant and you have a great lunch business that gets people lining up at the door for a great lunch, in a clean environment, at a fair value, then you too have a customer base to protect! A quick lunch can cost $5 to $8. One lost customer who was coming in twice a week with a friend would cost you $1000 to $1600 a year. The servers have something to lose as well! Tips for two people two times a week!

Extra Note!

This does not include the old saying that every lost customer will tell at least ten people!

Do the math!!

9: Workshops and Future Publications

I enjoy people and appreciate what people have invested in their businesses. I know you have to work hard to succeed, and that if you fail it is costly. That is why I have seen the need for the following help books and workshops.

Am I Fishing in the Right Pond?

This is a book on understanding your local business and promoting it to the full potential. If you are not content with the business, you have to *go out and get more!* This book explains the steps to local marketing and gives examples of making it work as well as numbers to show why we need to get the right promotions going in the right direction.

Did I Get the Right Person to Play this Part?

We have to make the right impression on our guests, but we also need to get the right person to make that impression. Most people hire the wrong people for a position, therefore they get the results that are unfavorable for their business. This book will help you understand the process of looking for the right person in the right places (the paper is often not that place). It will help you improve the interviewing process to make sure you are weeding out the wrong people and are aware when the right person comes in. We will highlight some areas like training and retaining employees.

There is profitability in hiring the right person the first time. We place a price on the hiring and training of an employee. If we replace that person weekly or monthly, what does it cost? (A lot.) A $1,200 investment on a new hire can cost $62,000 a year. That will affect the bottom line.

Other contents include:

- Why hire the right person for the job?

- Why are we always hiring? The need to or the opportunity to get better?

- The tipped employee!

WORKSHOPS (OR AS I LIKE TO CALL THEM, FUN SHOPS)

I like to call them Fun Shops because as a franchisee I liked learning how to make my business better and I liked having fun at doing this. So I developed a theory that if people have fun they retain more of the topics discussed.

If one of these topics has caught your attention, then why not share it with your employees? We offer Fun Shops that range from a few hours of training to a full day of fun and learning in a seminar form. Please call for schedules, availability, and pricing.

Our Customers Count, Inc. ~ Web Site Ourcustomerscount.com

10: Mission Statement:

To make all those in business that invest in their futures to be as successful as possible by understanding what their largest commodity truly is:

Their Customers!

To share this understanding with others in print and workshops alike!

Our Customers Count!

NOTES: